# HIP-HOP ARTISTS

# TYLER, THE CREATOR

## ALTERNATIVE HIP-HOP PRODUCER

BY MARIE JASKULKA

Essential Library

An Imprint of Abdo Publishing
abdobooks.com

## ABDOBOOKS.COM

Published by Abdo Publishing, a division of ABDO, PO Box 398166, Minneapolis, Minnesota 55319. Copyright © 2020 by Abdo Consulting Group, Inc. International copyrights reserved in all countries. No part of this book may be reproduced in any form without written permission from the publisher. Essential Library™ is a trademark and logo of Abdo Publishing.

Printed in the United States of America, North Mankato, Minnesota.
092019
012020

THIS BOOK CONTAINS RECYCLED MATERIALS

Cover Photo: Daniel Boczarski/Redferns/Getty Images
Interior Photos: Jack Plunkett/Invision/AP/Rex Features, 4; MACH Photos/Shutterstock Images, 7; Austin Humphreys/Austin American-Statesman/AP Images, 8; Josh Brasted/WireImage/Getty Images, 11; Alex Sudea/Rex Features, 14, 49; Chris Polk/FilmMagic/Getty Images, 17; Josh Brasted/FilmMagic/Getty Images, 19; imageSPACE/Rex Features, 22; Tim Mosenfelder/Getty Images Entertainment/Getty Images, 24; Chelsea Lauren/WireImage/Getty Images, 27, 74; Maggie Boyd/Sipa USA/AP Images, 30; Chris Pizzello/AP/Rex Features, 33; Stewart Cook/Rex Features, 34–35; Johnny Nunez/WireImage/Getty Images, 38–39; Scott Dudelson/Getty Images Entertainment/Getty Images, 41; Matt Sayles/AP/Rex Features, 44–45; Taylor Hill/WireImage/Governors Ball Music Festival/Getty Images, 46; Wes And Alex/Variety/Rex Features, 54–55; Bennett Raglin/BET/Getty Images Entertainment/Getty Images, 58–59; Eric Charbonneau/Invision/AP Images, 60; Rich Fury/Invision/AP Images, 62–63; Justin Ng/Retna/Photoshot/Newscom, 67; Nick Pickles/Redferns/Getty Images, 68; MAF/Emelie Andersson/WENN/Newscom, 70; Chelsea Lauren/Variety/Rex Features, 73; Vittorio Zunino Celotto/Gucci/Getty Images Entertainment/Getty Images, 77; John Shearer/Invision/AP Images, 78; Nicholas Hunt/Getty Images Entertainment/Getty Images, 80, 87; Robb Cohen/Invision/AP Images, 84–85; Anthony Behar/Sipa USA/AP Images, 90; Maggie Boyd/Sipa USA/Newscom, 92; Stephane Cardinale/Corbis Entertainment/Getty Images, 95; Paul Zimmerman/Rex Features, 96

Editor: Megan Ellis
Series Designer: Laura Graphenteen

## LIBRARY OF CONGRESS CONTROL NUMBER: 2019942109
## PUBLISHER'S CATALOGING-IN-PUBLICATION DATA

Names: Jaskulka, Marie, author.
Title: Tyler, the Creator: alternative hip-hop producer / by Marie Jaskulka
Other title: alternative hip-hop producer
Description: Minneapolis, Minnesota : Abdo Publishing, 2020 | Series: Hip-hop artists | Includes online resources and index.
Identifiers: ISBN 9781532190223 (lib. bdg.) | ISBN 9781532176074 (ebook)
Subjects: LCSH: Tyler, the Creator, 1991- (Tyler Okonma)--Juvenile literature. | Rap (Music)--Juvenile literature. | Songwriters--Juvenile literature. | Sound recording executives and producers--Juvenile literature. | Singers--Juvenile literature. | African American fashion designers--Juvenile literature.
Classification: DDC 782.421649--dc23

# CONTENTS

**CHAPTER ONE**
**RIOT IN AUSTIN, TEXAS**
4

**CHAPTER TWO**
**EARLY LIFE**
14

**CHAPTER THREE**
**THE EARLY DAYS OF ODD FUTURE**
24

**CHAPTER FOUR**
**"THE VIDEO OF 2011"**
34

**CHAPTER FIVE**
**BRANCHING INTO NEW PROJECTS**
46

**CHAPTER SIX**
**TYLER TRIES TO GROW**
60

**CHAPTER SEVEN**
***CHERRY BOMB* AND THE DOCUMENTARY**
70

**CHAPTER EIGHT**
***FLOWER BOY* AND *IGOR***
80

**CHAPTER NINE**
**THE FUTURE OF TYLER**
90

| | |
|---|---|
| TIMELINE | 98 |
| ESSENTIAL FACTS | 100 |
| GLOSSARY | 102 |
| ADDITIONAL RESOURCES | 104 |
| SOURCE NOTES | 106 |
| INDEX | 110 |
| ABOUT THE AUTHOR | 112 |

## Chapter ONE

# RIOT IN AUSTIN, TEXAS

Tyler Okonma stood on the stage of the Scoot Inn, a small club in East Austin, Texas, during the 2014 South by Southwest (SXSW) music festival. The audience screamed and cheered with excitement. Okonma, known by his stage name Tyler, the Creator, was in demand. Fans had overflowed the venue, just trying to catch a glimpse of the artist. Tyler was a 23-year-old rapper from Los Angeles, California. Many people who couldn't get inside tried to hear the show, which was sponsored by skateboarding magazine *Thrasher*, from outside the gates.

Tensions ran high in the crowd at his Thursday afternoon performance, as well as among the security officers and employees of the venue. Just one night before, on March 13, a man had plowed his car through a barricade at SXSW, killing four people and injuring many others who were waiting in line for Tyler's show. The driver

> Tyler was scheduled to perform three times at South by Southwest in 2014.

had been attempting to evade police. The incident cast a shadow over the ten-day music festival. Shortly after the accident occurred, Tyler had tweeted, "Show Isn't Happening. Something Sad Happened. I'm bummed."[1]

But when fans could not get into Tyler's Thursday afternoon performance, the young rapper known for his attention-getting antics encouraged the crowd to find a way in.

According to police reports, Tyler encouraged his fans to start a riot. His manager later referred to it as a "punk rock moment" from an otherwise law-abiding person. But according to police, Tyler allegedly said into the microphone, "All y'all outside the gates, y'all push through." Other people reported him saying, "I want all of you to run in here at the same time."[2]

## SOUTH BY SOUTHWEST

South by Southwest (SXSW) is a conference and collection of festivals that takes place in Austin, Texas, each year. It was founded in 1987. SXSW brings artists, musicians, comedians, and technology professionals together. Attendees of the festivals can watch movie premieres, discover new music, and participate in improv comedy sketches. Recording artists who have performed at SXSW include Tyler, the Creator, Questlove, and Billie Eilish.

**SXSW events happen all over the city of Austin, including on city streets.**

Some of the fans listened to Tyler. They began chanting "Push! Push! Push!" as a large stream of fans busted through the gates.³ The fans pushed through security guards and employees, pouring into the already full venue. Inside the club was chaos. A bartender had to protect a woman from being trampled in the crowd. While the bartender helped the woman, a fan punched him in the face.

In an attempt to stop the riot, an employee abruptly cut off the music. The fans grew angrier. The staff, worried about making the situation worse, restarted the music, and Tyler rapped to the raucous, oversized audience, finishing his set.

**The crowd at Tyler's show pushed through the barrier to get inside the venue.**

After the show, Tyler seemed pleased, tweeting, "THRASHER SHOW WAS GREAT! HAPPY EVERYONE GOT IN. I PLAY PANDORA TONIGHT AT 1AM COME!!!"

However, not everyone was pleased with the show. Some thought the rapper showed poor judgment, given the events of the night before. Tyler canceled the show he had scheduled for Friday night, tweeting by way of explanation, "I DONT WANT TO CAUSE ANY TROUBLE, SOME ARE MAKING ME OUT TO BE A BAD GUY, SO IM NOT DOING ANY SHOWS TONIGHT."[4]

On Saturday, as Tyler waited to board a plane to his next show in Dallas, Texas, police approached him at the Austin-Bergstrom Airport. Officers arrested him for inciting a riot. This is a class A misdemeanor, which meant that Tyler could go to jail for his actions if proven guilty. The police accused Tyler of purposely starting the trouble with the words he'd called to the crowd outside. If convicted, the artist faced a maximum of one year in jail and a $4,000 fine.[5]

While prosecutors maintained that the charges were justified, many others argued that the charges were overblown and unfair. Perry Minton, Tyler's lawyer, explained, "I personally believe there was no riot, and I feel that in the end, the Travis County attorney saw there was

**Tyler continued to tour in 2014, even after the events at SXSW.**

## THE RISE TO FAME

Tyler has struggled with the way his rapid rise to fame changed his life in unexpected ways. In a 2011 interview with internet music magazine *Spin*, he commented on people who say that "most of [his] songs are about how he can't handle fame and it's too much." Tyler addressed those people, saying, "I want *you* to be f****** 20 years old and wake up one day with f****** thousands of dollars in your bank account. . . . And not being able to go skate . . . because 40 motherf****** wanna take pictures all of a sudden." Tyler has said that he tries to stay grounded and not let the fame or money get to his head. He often watches TV and plays video games to de-stress. Tyler added, "I just have so much and I'm 20 years old, when most people have to worry about their next term paper. . . . I just try to smile. It could all be worse."[8]

never any intent on the part of Tyler to incite anything harmful or dangerous."[6] His lawyers had him out of jail the same night.

## REPERCUSSIONS

Although Tyler had no prior arrests on his record, he did have a reputation for starting trouble. Just one month before the SXSW incident, Tyler and his group of fellow musicians and artists in the hip-hop collective Odd Future had to cancel their gig at Eminem's Rapture festival when New Zealand immigration officials labeled them a "public threat."[7] The government refused to grant them

> "Youth is something I never wanna take for granted. I just want to smile and live life."[10]
>
> – Tyler, the Creator

## TYLER'S ASTHMA

Tyler has severe asthma. He's often seen using his inhaler while running around the stage during his action-packed shows. He also experiences coughing fits sometimes when being interviewed. Tyler has a tattoo of a guardian angel inhaler on his thigh to represent his life with asthma.

work visas to enter the country. The officials in New Zealand cited a different violent incident that happened in 2011 in Boston, Massachusetts, as one of their reasons.

To further confuse the situation, people suggested that Tyler's arrest was somehow connected to the unrelated fatal accident from outside his earlier show. The confusion led Tyler to clarify via tweet, "Dear You, That Tragedy That Happened Has Absolutly [sic] NOTHING To Do With The Show At Thrasher At A Different Location A Day Later. . . . So Please Stop Going Out Of Your Way To Mention The Tragedy And Tie Me To It, Thats Not Cool And It Bums Me Out."[9]

Leading up to SXSW, Tyler and his fellow creators in Odd Future had been dealing with a lot of blowback for their music. People complained that their music glorified violence and the mistreatment of women. But, Tyler argued, that wasn't his style at all. He was just a creative oddball who many kids related to, and many parents and authority figures didn't understand him.

# EARLY LIFE

Chapter TWO

Tyler Gregory Okonma was born on March 6, 1991, in Los Angeles, California. He grew up in the Ladera Heights and Hawthorne neighborhoods with his mother, Bonita Smith, and his sister, Lynda. Tyler never knew his father or any grandfathers, a fact that he rapped about in many of his early songs. Smith, a social worker, wanted to expose Tyler to what went on around him and in the world. She said, "I want him to know what's in the real world. I don't want him to be sheltered."[1]

In interviews and articles, Tyler often talks about how he felt different from his classmates as a child. He felt like an outsider. Instead of playing with toys, Tyler was interested in reading the liner notes on his favorite albums. His classmates made fun of him because when he was nine years old, he listened to R&B band Jamiroquai, which was not popular among his friends. He also believes that his hyperactivity and offbeat sense of humor meant that many of his friends and classmates didn't understand him. His black classmates called him "Whiteboy" because

Even during his first performances, Tyler was known for his onstage antics while rapping.

> Tyler looked up to professional skater Kareem Campbell.

he enjoyed skateboarding and genres of music that his classmates did not listen to.[2]

Tyler also had some behavioral problems at an early age. In fifth grade, Tyler met with a therapist to help him deal with anger issues and violent tendencies. However, he was also incredibly intelligent. He was placed into school programs for gifted children. Tyler directed some of his anger and energy into hobbies such as skateboarding and music.

Tyler says that he often looked for male role models in the media because he had very few in his real life. In the sixth grade, he noticed that there were some black skateboarders who were famous, such as Kareem Campbell. At age 12, Tyler got his first skateboard. Without anyone to teach him how to skateboard, he learned to ride it by copying what he saw in the video game *Tony Hawk's Pro Skater 4*.

Around the same time, Tyler began using Reason. Reason is a music production program that allows people to create,

> "I was a black skater kid. I liked . . . Good Charlotte and Kenny G, and I was black. And I went to school with a bunch of black kids so they kinda swayed away from me."[3]
>
> – Tyler, the Creator

## TYLER'S MOM AND HIS LYRICS

Tyler often sings the praises of his mother, who raised him on her own. Some fans wonder what his mother thinks of the violent images in some of his lyrics. For example, some of Tyler's raps contain lyrics with references to sexual assault, violence, and homophobia. But according to Tyler, his mother does not mind the violent lyrics. "She looks past that," he said. "She just sees her son onstage enjoying his life after the circumstances that he's had in the past couple of years."[4] In 2011, Tyler even moved in with his mother again for a brief period of time.

edit, and mix their own songs. Tyler also began teaching himself how to play piano. He looked up to black musicians in the public eye, such as Pharrell Williams, André 3000, and Kanye West. Tyler appreciated their outside-the-box, innovative approach to creating music, as well as their entrepreneurial skills. He also liked that Williams and West were confident about their offbeat, quirky style and music. They had made careers out of music production, online videos, fashion lines, and public art. They weren't just making music; they were creating experiences.

> "My favorite class was art because there were no rules. . . . You can make whatever you want. That's the freedom I get from making things. That's why I like drawing it out, because my mind can go anywhere."[5]
> 
> – Tyler, the Creator

André 3000 performed for many years as half of the hip-hop duo Outkast.

## GETTING HIS START

When Tyler was 16 years old, his mother moved to Sacramento, California. Tyler stayed back in Los Angeles with his grandmother in the Ladera Heights neighborhood. Most nights, he slept on his grandmother's couch or on her floor. While she supported Tyler, he also created a close-knit group of friends who would often

## YOUNG TYLER'S INFLUENCES

Tyler got a copy of Outkast's *Speakerboxxx/The Love Below* when he was 12, and he fell in love with the double album. He loved how it experimented with unusual beats and sounds. Many of his songs have been compared to the sound of André 3000. At Media Art Academy, a teacher called Tyler a "miniature André."[6] One critic noted that the sound of Tyler's 2019 album *IGOR* could be described as the spiritual successor to some of André 3000's work.

Tyler also often speaks of Pharrell Williams as an inspiration. On the tenth anniversary of the release of Williams's album *In My Mind*, Tyler wrote a tribute to the album. He said that the song "You Can Do It Too" inspired him to create Odd Future. Tyler explains, "I [believed] I could have any car I wanted, any types of stones, marry who I want, make the music I wanted to and do all these amazing things by just being who I am."[7] Williams and Tyler have since collaborated on several songs.

hang out and share meals together. He met many of them on the social media platform MySpace. Tyler made videos of himself and his friends hanging out, playing music, and skateboarding together. Tyler also spent a lot of time posting about music on blogs such as Hypebeast, where he connected with music fans and friends around the world.

Tyler attended many different schools while he was growing up, because he and his family moved a lot. For a while in high school, he attended Media Art Academy in Hawthorne, California. The charter school also goes by the nickname "Hip Hop High," because students can use state-of-the-art music production equipment as part of their classes. Music production is one way the school engages students in learning. Hip Hop High was Tyler's eleventh school in eleven years, but it was also a place where the budding artist could bloom.

By the time he attended Media Art Academy, Tyler had already begun to develop his signature music style and gravelly, raspy voice. At the time, a reporter who was writing a story about Media Art Academy described Tyler's music as a "resplendent, psychedelic vision of street fashion gone haywire."[8] While at Media Art Academy, Tyler

"I was 17 and 18, I didn't think that stuff I was writing would matter."[9]
— Tyler, the Creator

### MUSIC TASTES

Early on, one way that Tyler, the Creator and Odd Future made themselves stand out was by revealing their tastes for eclectic music. They weren't embarrassed to say they liked non–hip-hop artists such as Kenny G. One of their favorite obscure artists was James Pants. Pants was once a DJ for a black nationalist rap group. He released his debut album, *Welcome*, in 2008. Pants said the album was part of a musical genre that he called "fresh beat," which was a mix of "80s boogie, synth experiments, garage rock, and much more."[10]

> Tyler's interest in eclectic fashion inspired him to create the magazine *Odd Future*.

envisioned a magazine called *Odd Future* that would show off his and his friends' designs. It focused on three areas: music, fashion, and skateboarding.

According to Lionel Boyce, Tyler's friend and writing partner, Tyler's high school classmates knew he was a great performer. He didn't talk about his music, but people were starting to listen. While he was still in high school, Tyler had no idea how close he was to becoming the star he dreamed of being. The friends Tyler made during high school were not just stand-ins for his family; they were also partners in his creations. Tyler's friend Domo Genesis used to come to Tyler's house to record early versions of songs on his computer. Together with some of their friends, they formed the hip-hop collective Odd Future.

# THE EARLY DAYS OF ODD FUTURE

Chapter THREE

After high school, Tyler enrolled in community college to make his mom happy. He planned to study film production. However, after attending classes for only four days, he began skipping school to work on his videos and music.

Tyler began vlogging, or video blogging, before the genre took off on YouTube. He documented his everyday life and activities in YouTube videos. The first video uploaded to his channel, titled "Normal Day," is under five minutes long. Footage shows Tyler skateboarding around a mall parking lot, playing with sound equipment in an electronics store while his friend dances, and drinking Starbucks with his friends.

The videos on Tyler's channel featured the members of Odd Future: Left Brain, Hodgy Beats, Matt Martians, Jasper Dolphin, Casey Veggies, and Brandun DeShay.

> Tyler performed his first shows while touring with other members of Odd Future.

Tyler summed up Odd Future in an interview: "Just music lovers who make what they love. . . . It's like a religion. It's a lot of us that grew up together and have been friends for years. Skaters, musicians, artist[s], college students . . . just kids who have something in common."[1] The band's full name was long and nonsensical: Odd Future Wolf Gang Kill Them All, or OFWGKTA. Sometimes it changed, depending on the day. The members showed that they had an irreverent sense of humor and didn't take themselves too seriously. The teens goofed off and had a good time in front of the camera. But when Syd Bennett joined Odd Future, the group moved closer toward the dream of making music.

## SYD BENNETT CONTROVERSY

Syd Bennett often receives criticism for being part of Odd Future. People did not like that she was a lesbian who was associated with lyrics that were violent toward women and people in the LGBTQ community. Though Bennett's feelings were hurt by the backlash, the experience taught her to think more about her music before she released it. She said, "When you're young making art before you start thinking too much is when you come up with the best ideas. . . . When you put those ideas out, all the judgment definitely makes you think twice."[2] In the past, Bennett has questioned whether she was used by other members of Odd Future to justify their homophobic lyrics. However, Bennett insists that Odd Future is not a homophobic group.

**Bennett helped Odd Future produce its first songs and start getting noticed by music industry professionals.**

Bennett had also started making music at a young age. She used the music program GarageBand and a few pieces of audio equipment to create a small music studio in her bedroom. Bennett advertised this studio online as a place for local young musicians to record their music. Soon after Bennett expanded to a larger studio, she met Tyler and the rest of Odd Future through MySpace. Bennett was a fan of their music, so she did not charge Odd Future to use her studio. In exchange, they made her a member of the group and began calling her Syd Tha Kyd.

However, many of Odd Future's early songs contained lyrics with controversial themes. The members used jokes that were homophobic, misogynistic, and violent. They also rapped about wanting to sexually assault women. When Bennett's parents heard Odd Future's music for the first time, they banned the group from using Bennett's studio.

When Odd Future first posted its music online, it didn't get much of a response. Again, Bennett stepped in to help. She noticed that other artists and bands usually send out press releases to blogs and magazines when they release new music. Bennett set up a fake

### THE INTERNET BAND

Two members of Odd Future, Syd Bennett and Matt Martians, formed the band the Internet. They create funky, jazzy dance music, and they're characterized by an always rotating roster. The band's first album, *Purple Naked Ladies*, was the first to be released on the Odd Future Records label. In 2017, the band took a break so the members could focus on their solo projects. In 2018, they reunited to create their fourth album.

> "It's a weird situation when the first songs you write as a kid become who you are to people."[3]
> – Tyler, the Creator

public relations firm to send press releases to the same outlets. She built a website that looked similar to those of music magazines *Fader* and *Pitchfork*. Soon, blogs and digital magazines began to talk more about Odd Future's releases.

## FIRST ALBUMS

As the videos and mixtapes became more popular, new people started appearing in Odd Future projects. Rappers Frank Ocean and Earl Sweatshirt were two early additions to the group. Odd Future continued to put out content, and music industry professionals took notice. Many people felt that Odd Future was about to blow up in the music world.

Odd Future created music for fun, which was likely how its members were able to produce so much of it so quickly. Odd Future's first full-length mixtape, *The Odd Future*

### OTHER JOBS

While they created music, Tyler and some of the other members of Odd Future also interned at a clothing store called Reserve in the Fairfax district of Los Angeles. For his work at Reserve, Tyler was paid in clothes. The managers at the store remember the guys pranking customers and practicing skateboard tricks in front of and even in the store. Tyler would often introduce himself to customers using fake names—a goof he also pulled in his videos.

> **Earl Sweatshirt became a member of Odd Future when he was a teenager.**

*Tape Vol. 1*, was released on November 16, 2008. Between 2008 and 2011, the group released 12 albums, as well as various singles. All of its content was free to download on the social media platform Tumblr. The group kept its new fans happy by constantly posting new free music and engaging with fans where they hung out—on social media platforms like Tumblr and Reddit.

Tyler released *Bastard*, his first full-length solo album, for free on December 25, 2009. The album begins with Tyler playing the character of Dr. TC, who is prepared to discipline Tyler for misbehaving in class. Tyler then raps about absent fathers in a song that touches on what appeared to be his drive for creating music—an intense, explosive anger. In one song, Tyler raps, "I feel we're more talented than 40-year-old rappers talking about Gucci / when they have kids they haven't seen in years."[4]

Music industry insiders were starting to gain interest in the creative collective. Music website *Pitchfork* ranked the album, completely produced and released by Tyler, among the Top 50 albums of 2010.[5] The success of *Bastard* brought more attention to all of the members of Odd Future. Record executive Dave Airaudi sent the song "French" by Odd Future to Christian Clancy. Clancy

## CHRISTIAN AND KELLY CLANCY

Management team and husband and wife Christian and Kelly Clancy were often called the stand-in parents of the Odd Future members. They met while working at Interscope Records. Also included in their family is the couple's daughter, Chloe, who can be seen in lots of photos of Odd Future's early touring days. Chloe was a toddler when her parents met the group, and she is sometimes referred to as the youngest member of Odd Future.

was a former executive at Interscope Records who had worked on Eminem's *The Marshall Mathers LP*. He found the music inspiring, and he met with the members of Odd Future shortly after. Kelly Clancy, Christian Clancy's wife, explained the early allure of Odd Future, saying that Tyler's creativity and innovation "inspired kids because before, everything sounded and looked the same."[6]

Christian and Kelly Clancy began to manage the group. Tyler was skeptical about involving outside managers. However, he was sold after a life-threatening event in 2010. Christian was driving Odd Future to the group's first paying gig when they almost got into a car accident. Christian swerved off the road to avoid an oncoming car, and the young group made it to their show. Afterward, Christian took the band out to a diner and paid their bill.

Odd Future members liked to clown around, both on YouTube and at events they attended together, such as the MTV Video Music Awards (VMAs).

Tyler soon realized, "This the dude."[7] Christian and Kelly not only understood the magic of Odd Future, but they also thought the band had the potential to make it big.

## Chapter FOUR
# "THE VIDEO OF 2011"

While Odd Future had experienced some level of success before 2011, the group really came onto the scene when Tyler released the song "Yonkers" in February. Tyler had recently signed a one-album record deal with XL Recordings, an indie record company known for a catalog of talented artists such as Adele and Beck. XL Recordings prides itself on only signing innovative musical acts that the label's management personally likes. It seemed like a great fit for Tyler and his music. On his signing with the company, Tyler commented, "They have awesome artists. It's all the weirdos in one place, getting out to the rest of the weirdos in the world, so it's all cool."[1]

The song "Yonkers" was Tyler's most popular song to date. *Pitchfork* called it "the best thing any OF affiliate has produced to date . . . the perfect distillation of what they do well." The song opens with the line, "I'm a f******

Tyler's song "Yonkers" helped him win an award for Best New Artist in 2011.

walking paradox, no I'm not," which hooked listeners from the start.² "Yonkers" is three minutes of dark lyrics sung in Tyler's deep, raspy voice and backed by a steady hypnotic beat. In 2011, *Pitchfork* named "Yonkers" a best new track. Contributor Zach Kelly wrote:

> "Yonkers" is . . . the perfect distillation of what they [Odd Future] do well. The beat (produced by Tyler) lurches uncomfortably, sounding like someone failing to dead start an engine, and it's a perfectly grim platform for Tyler's words. He appears here as funny, irreverent, and frightening as we've seen him.³

Unlike previous songs put out by Odd Future, the video for "Yonkers" was more professional. Christian Clancy brought in popular music video director Anthony Mandler. Mandler introduced Tyler to all of the tricks and technologies available to professional videographers. He also introduced him to other seasoned music production professionals who could take his art to the next level.

Tyler was only 19 years old when he self-directed the video for "Yonkers" under the alias Wolf Haley, one of the alter egos he uses in his videos and songs with Odd Future. The black-and-white video features Tyler sitting on a stool, rapping directly into the camera while a cockroach crawls around his hands. Eventually, Tyler eats the cockroach before puking it back up. At the end of the video, Tyler is shown inflicting self-harm. Many thought this imagery was shocking, even for Tyler. But according to Zach Kelly, "At the heart of the clip is Tyler's remarkable performance—one so convincingly maddened that the shock tactics barely register, and all that is left is the face of a twisted, wildly clever child of the digital age."[4]

## THE VIDEO RECEPTION

The video was an unexpected success. On February 23, Kanye West called it "The Video of 2011" on Twitter. The video was nominated at the MTV Video Music Awards (VMAs) for Best New Artist and Video of the Year. The video also led to online

### EARL SWEATSHIRT

Earl Sweatshirt, real name Thebe Kgositsile, was just 16 years old in 2010 when he created his first mixtape, *Earl*, with Tyler. The release gathered Sweatshirt attention from critics and fans. However, Sweatshirt's mother became worried about his behavior. She sent him away to a boarding school in Samoa. Sweatshirt could not record music with Odd Future for over a year.

During his disappearance, Odd Future did not explain Sweatshirt's whereabouts. However, group members would chant "Free Earl!"[5] at their concerts to keep the mystery alive. In interviews, Odd Future members dodged the question, saying that Sweatshirt was either dead or on vacation. Sweatshirt returned to Los Angeles and rejoined Odd Future in 2012.

> **Tyler's popularity grew quickly after releasing "Yonkers."**

discussions about its deeper meaning and purpose. Tyler begged his fans, "Stop trying to f****** find meaning into it. I just wanted to f****** do it."[6]

Just a week after "Yonkers" rocked the music world, Odd Future made its national television debut on *Late Night with Jimmy Fallon*. Tyler and Hodgy Beats performed the single "Sandwitches" from Tyler's upcoming album *Goblin*. Tyler wore a green ski mask and Hodgy wore a black ski mask for most of the performance. The stage was covered in gnomes, and fog machines gave it a spooky vibe. A young girl with stringy black hair who was wearing a hospital gown roamed the stage behind Tyler and Hodgy. Tyler and Hodgy raged around the stage and sang into the faces of the other guests. At the end of the outrageous performance, Tyler jumped on host Jimmy Fallon's back as the crowd erupted in excitement.

For months, the members of Odd Future had found success on YouTube and Tumblr,

In addition to rapping with Tyler on several songs from *Goblin*, Hodgy also had a solo career and performed on other Odd Future tracks.

"Last night, the L.A. rap crew Odd Future made their television debut on *Late Night with Jimmy Fallon*, and pretty much proved in an instant why people can't shut up about them."[8]

— Ryan Schreiber, *Pitchfork*

but they did not know how more mainstream audiences would react to their act. The next day, reviews of the performances congratulated Tyler and Hodgy Beats on an "absolutely insane performance."[7]

## ODD FUTURE RECORDS

With the runaway success of Odd Future, big labels were fighting to sign the collective of performers to a standard record deal. In April 2011, Christian Clancy helped the members of Odd Future create their own record label, Odd Future Records, which operated under Sony Records. Under

### TUMBLR CHANGE

Critics noted that 2011 is the year the band's Tumblr account shifted. At first, the band posted only gritty, blurry real-life images. But soon, members began to post staged photos with famous rappers and images from behind the scenes at media appearances. The success of "Yonkers" was a culmination of all the prep work Tyler had done leading up to that moment.

## FRANK OCEAN

Ocean already had a record deal with Def Jam Records when he joined Odd Future. Ocean has experienced a meteoric rise to fame since his days with the collective. He won Grammys for Best Urban Contemporary Album and Best Rap/Sung Collaboration in 2012. As of 2019, Ocean had received seven Grammy nominations. However, Ocean did not submit his 2016 album, *Blonde*, for consideration to the Recording Academy, which judges and hosts the Grammys. In an interview with the *New York Times*, Ocean stated, "[The Grammys] certainly has nostalgic importance. It just doesn't seem to be representing very well for people who come from where I come from, and hold down what I hold down."[9]

the deal, Sony would publish the records of all of the Odd Future artists, with the exception of Frank Ocean, who was already signed to another label. The collective's debut release under the label was *The OF Tape, Vol. 2*, released on March 20, 2012.

Odd Future signed a deal with Sony Music that worked in the artists' favor. The contract gave them complete creative control over their projects, including release dates and cover art. Manager Christian Clancy explained why the band waited: "[It] allows the group to 'sign themselves' to their own company. . . . Sony know[s] that it's in everyone's best

> "[Odd Future] was the punk rock of that generation. It's YouTube and beats instead of guitars."[10]
> – Mark Williams, the record executive who signed Odd Future to Sony in 2011

interest to maintain the group's authenticity and control. They built it, they deserve it."[11]

Only one month after he signed the deal with Sony, Tyler released *Goblin*, his first full-length studio album, on May 10, 2011. He was only 20 years old. The *New York Times* called *Goblin*, "spiteful, internal, confident, vitriolic, vividly bruised stuff, a shocking . . . album that bears little resemblance to contemporary hip-hop."[12] The album's slogan, "Kill people! Burn s***! F*** school!" would become a popular mantra to yell at Odd Future concerts.

At the VMAs that year, Tyler, the Creator took home his first award, with his mom by his side in the audience.

## POETIC ROOTS

Earl Sweatshirt's father is Keorapetse Kgositsile, the 2006 poet laureate of South Africa. During apartheid, a time when black and white people were segregated in South Africa, Kgositsile lived in exile. He traveled to Chicago, Illinois, where he met Earl's mother. When the marriage fell apart, Kgositsile moved back to South Africa. When he heard of his son's fame, he said he hadn't known his son was famous, explaining, "When he feels that he's got something to share with me, he'll do that. And until then I will not impose myself on him just because the world talks of him." Kgositsile is not a fan of the kind of commercial rap Earl Sweatshirt creates, saying, "I really don't think it's about anything of relevance, socially, other than young people saying they're hurt."[13]

**Other members of Odd Future celebrated onstage with Tyler at the MTV VMAs.**

He won the Best New Artist award over fellow nominees Wiz Khalifa, Foster the People, Big Sean, and Kreayshawn. Tyler commented, "I wanted this s*** since I was nine. I'm about to cry."[14] As he walked up to accept his award, Tyler jumped up onto the stage. His Odd Future friends

rushed up to stand by his side, hug him, and pat him on the back. During his speech, the camera cut to his mother in the audience, waving, crying, and reaching to the sky in happiness.

"I put my personal life into my music, and I do it in my clothes, too."[1]
– Tyler, the Creator

## Chapter FIVE
# BRANCHING INTO NEW PROJECTS

As Tyler and the rest of Odd Future gained popularity for their music and videos, many fans looked to the group for another source of inspiration: their sense of style. Odd Future had always dressed in their favorite skater brands, such as Vans, Supreme, and Thrasher, which made them stand out visually from other hip-hop artists. Fans wanted to look, act, and sound just like Odd Future. Companies in various industries, including the skater fashion brands that Odd Future loved, courted the young artists, hungry to collaborate.

Manager Christian Clancy worked with Tyler to brainstorm new projects and ideas for Odd Future to tackle. They spent a lot of time on Tyler's grandmother's couch, going over Tyler's ideas and sketches. According to

Tyler used his platform as a rapper to introduce fans to his fashion label.

**Odd Future merchandise featured wacky designs with the group's initials and logos.**

Clancy, he helped Tyler translate his off-the-wall style into something that other people would want to partner with.

## FASHION

In November 2011, Odd Future opened a pop-up store that sold mostly T-shirts designed by Tyler. The store eventually became a permanent fixture on Fairfax Avenue in Los Angeles, near a clothing store where Tyler and some other members of Odd Future had worked before they became famous. As the store grew, Tyler stepped back on some of the creative decisions and let his bandmates work with producers and cover artists.

At just 20 years old, Tyler founded his own fashion label, Golf Wang. The name was a play on "Wolf Gang" from the band's full name, Odd Future Wolf Gang Kill

### CHARITABLE GIVING

In 2013, Tyler donated some Odd Future clothes to people experiencing homelessness. However, he did not go through typical shelters or other charities. Instead, Tyler drove to a street corner in Los Angeles with a box of brightly colored streetwear items. While his friends filmed him, Tyler dropped the box of clothes on the side of the road. He yelled, "It's a big a** box of fresh a** clothes right here if any of you . . . need it."[2] Tyler then dropped more boxes of clothes before driving away.

Them All. The Odd Future store on Fairfax sold Golf Wang clothes as well as other Odd Future designs from the rest of the band. In December 2011, Tyler published his first lookbook. It was a magazine filled with glossy images of Odd Future members posing with their skateboards while wearing Golf Wang designs.

The Odd Future store consistently sold out of its offerings in stores, online, and on tour. When new merch became available on tour, fans waited in line for the hard-to-nab pieces. Golf Wang started with T-shirts, hats, and hoodies, but soon it grew into a huge collection.

In 2012, Tyler collaborated with Vans on a line of Vans Old Skool sneakers, which had been worn by skaters since the 1970s. Tyler's first line of Vans came in four different colors and had the words "Golf" and "Wang"

### TYLER AND GOLFING

While Tyler uses the word *golf* on many clothing items that he designs, he doesn't like the sport. According to Tyler, "The word just looks sick." In an interview with *Golf Digest*, Tyler claimed that golf is actually his "least favorite sport."[3] However, Tyler plays a character on the TV show *Loiter Squad* who loves golf. On an episode of the show, Tyler's character Thurnis Hayley says, "I don't take care of none of my kids. You know why? 'Cause golfin' is more important."[4]

stitched into the back of either shoe. Tyler created several other designs for collaborations with Vans over the next three years. However, in 2015, he started his own shoe company called Golf le Fleur*. According to Tyler, "I still love Vans, but I wanted to be more in control. . . . And I'm over getting royalty checks; I don't want to get a certain percent for something that I thought of. So why not start my own shoe company?"[5]

Singer Pharrell Williams introduced Tyler to executives at Converse in 2016. The shoe company wanted an innovative collaboration like Kanye had done with Adidas. Converse partnered with Tyler for a line of Golf le Fleur* Converse shoes. The first design, a limited-edition powder-blue low-top basketball shoe called the One Star, dropped on July 10, 2017, and sold out quickly. Soon, Converse was rolling out full collections by Tyler, the Creator each year. As usual, Tyler wasn't content just creating shoes; he also provided direction on how the promotional materials should look.

> "When I make clothes, there's not really, like, deeper meaning. I just make what I want to wear. . . . You gotta make what you know."[6]
> – Tyler, the Creator

## OCEAN COMES OUT

In early 2012, Odd Future member Ocean was poised to release his debut album, *Channel Orange*, when people at a listening party commented on the fact that the lead single, "Thinking About You," seemed to reference a male lover. In the song, Ocean raps, "My eyes don't shed tears, but boy, they pour when/I'm thinkin' 'bout you." In another Odd Future song, released in May 2012, Ocean raps, "I'm hi and I'm bi, wait, I mean I'm straight."[9]

Hip-hop blogs began speculating about Ocean's sexuality. In July 2012, Ocean addressed the rumors on his personal Tumblr. He wrote candidly about a relationship that he'd had with a man when he was 19 years old. Some people were nervous how other members in Odd Future would react to Ocean coming out of the closet, based on the homophobic lyrics in some of their earlier songs. However, Tyler was one of the first people to tweet his support: "My big brother finally f***** did that. Proud of that n**** cause I know that s*** is difficult."[10]

## ODD FUTURE CARNIVAL

The members of Odd Future branched out in every direction. On September 30, 2012, Odd Future held the first OFWGKTA Carnival, a celebration of creativity in music, art, and fashion. Tyler curated the acts who performed. The first carnival lasted one day and was held in the parking lot of Club Nokia in Los Angeles. It featured "games, rides, prizes, and food hand-picked by Odd Future."[7] More than 2,000 people attended the first OFWGKTA Carnival, which many called Camp Flog Gnaw.[8] "Flog Gnaw" is yet another play on Wolf Gang.

In 2014, Tyler officially changed the name of the annual carnival to Camp Flog Gnaw. Then, in 2016, it turned into a two-day festival for which he curates all the musical acts and brings together art, food, and technology. Tyler employed his usual entrepreneurial savvy, presenting an opportunity for brands to market directly to his fans through sponsorships and partnerships. Kevin Wattles, the director of strategic partnerships at electronics company ZAGG, which was involved with Camp Flog Gnaw, said, "They [Odd Future] don't attract the typical music fans that attend just to see a show, their audience is more tech savvy, engaged and represents a free-spirited generation of fans."[11]

Many of the Odd Future members release new music at the annual festival. In 2018, planners moved the location of the carnival to Dodger Stadium. The event sold more than 40,000 tickets.[12]

## MOVING TO TELEVISION

Tyler and his friends were well-versed in the art of making goofy videos for social media. However, they had never created comedy videos professionally until the media company Cartoon Network heard about Odd Future. Tyler had been posting on Cartoon Network's

The 2016 Camp Flog Gnaw featured musical performances and many carnival rides for attendees to enjoy.

message boards for years, telling everyone who would listen that he'd have his own show one day. In 2012, that dream became a reality, when two executives for Adult Swim attended an Odd Future show at a nightclub in Los Angeles. The department produced videos aimed at teenagers and young adults for Cartoon Network. It was known for appealing to the same demographics as Odd

Future's videos with shows such as *Robot Chicken* and *Harvey Birdman*.

After the show, they met with Tyler and some other members of Odd Future. The execs remember the young artists standing up, slapping each other, and whispering during the meeting. One of them, Walter J. Newman, described their behavior as "what you'd normally never do in a meeting."[13] However, the executives liked Tyler and Odd Future. Adult Swim agreed to produce an Odd Future sketch comedy show called *Loiter Squad*.

Odd Future teamed up with a production company headed by Jeff Tremaine, who had directed other popular TV shows for MTV. Tremaine attempted to figure out what made Odd Future tick and replicate it in a way that would work for national television. Producers of the show would go on tour with Odd Future and create scenes that worked in whatever city they happened to be in. While all ten members of Odd Future made appearances on the show, it largely centered on Tyler. It premiered on March 25, 2012.

## GOLF MEDIA APP

In 2014, Cartoon Network let Tyler know they would be ending his Odd Future

### LIONEL AND TYLER'S COLLABORATION

Tyler's writing partner on *Loiter Squad* and *The Jellies* is Lionel Boyce. The writing team signed a first-look deal with Sony Pictures TV. In a first-look deal, that production company gets to see any of the artists' new show ideas. If Sony Pictures TV isn't interested, the artists can shop their show ideas elsewhere. On the signing of the deal, Lionel said, "Sony Pictures Television has been a hub for great television for many decades and we're excited to be a part of a place where we will have the resources to develop new ideas." Tyler added, "Tacos are great with bar-b-que sauce, I'm excited."[14]

sketch comedy show, *Loiter Squad*. The show had run for three seasons, and Tyler thought the project was just heating up. Adult Swim suggested several other projects to Tyler and his writing partner, Lionel Boyce. Nothing sparked their interest.

Tyler and Boyce brainstormed ideas for new shows. They produced their own new cartoon called *The Jellies*. The show was about a pair of jellyfish parents and their adopted human child, Cornell. Cornell is shocked when he finds out that he was adopted. Cornell feels like an outsider among his jellyfish peers, so he sets off on an adventure to find himself.

Much like his partnership with Vans, Tyler wanted full creative control over his projects. In 2015, he started Golf Media as a way to get his content straight to his fans without restrictions. The app was available for download on smartphones. After a two-month free trial, users paid a $5 monthly subscription for a constant stream of original and Tyler-curated content, including articles, movies, music, videos, and links to merchandise. *The Jellies* made its debut

> "[Jellyfish are] smarter than us. . . . A lot of them don't die, they split into two and then they've got homies."[15]
> — Tyler, the Creator

**Tyler, *kneeling*, appeared with the Loiter Squad on the BET Network to promote the show in 2014.**

on the Golf Media app. Tyler called the app his "vision," saying, "It's not about the money for me. I wanted my own network. I wanted to do something cool. It's always about me doing something that I think is awesome."[16]

After Cartoon Network saw the success of the first season of *The Jellies* on the Golf Media app, executives

approached Tyler and Boyce. Adult Swim acquired the show and contracted the pair to write the second season. In 2018, Tyler announced that he would discontinue putting out content on the Golf Media app. However, *The Jellies* was still available to watch on Adult Swim.

# TYLER TRIES TO GROW

## Chapter SIX

Tyler released his second studio album, *Wolf*, on the Odd Future Records label on April 2, 2013. In typical Tyler fashion, he joked in interviews that "the beats are really bad. My raps have gotten worse."[2] Of course, he was just up to his normal antics. Many Odd Future members, including Hodgy Beats and Earl Sweatshirt, made appearances on the album. The songs on this album fused Tyler's abrasive lyrics with rich instrumental melodies. *Wolf* featured another appearance by fictional character Dr. TC, who first appeared on Tyler's album *Bastard*. Tyler released a deluxe version with a 24-page booklet and other pieces of merchandise. He also released the entire album for free on SoundCloud.

Critics gave the album great reviews. The album debuted at Number 3 on the US *Billboard* 200. *Pitchfork* commented on Tyler's obvious growth as a producer on

> Multiple hip-hop publications named *Wolf* one of the top albums of the year.

> Tyler performed songs from *Wolf* at the 2015 Coachella Valley Music and Arts Festival in Indio, California.

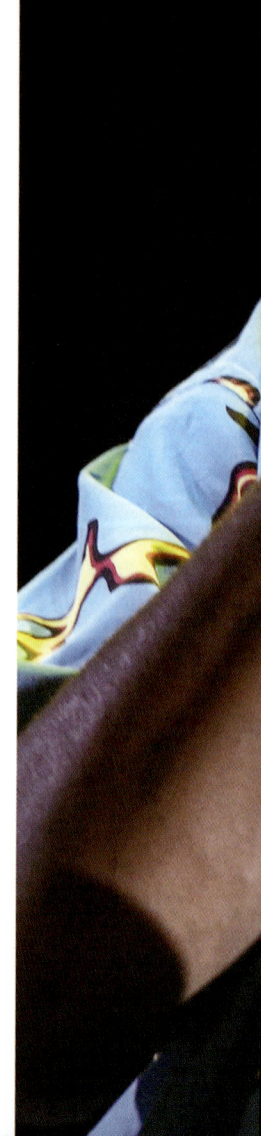

*Wolf*, as well as his growth as a songwriter, writing, "Wolf pulls back the curtain and reveal[s] the talented introvert behind the music."[3] In 2014, MTV nominated Tyler for a VMA for Best Art Direction for his video for "Tamale," which begins with the subtitle, "A visual interpretation of Tyler's mind."[4]

## FELICIA THE GOAT

Corporations continued to work with Tyler. In 2013, Pepsi hired Tyler to create an innovative ad campaign for Mountain Dew. Tyler worked on three digital commercials for the soda company. They featured a male goat named Felicia who was in love with Mountain Dew.

In the first commercial, a couple eating at a restaurant watches as Felicia bites and kicks at a waitress for not bringing him enough Mountain Dew. The second commercial shows Felicia getting pulled over by the police for speeding. When the

> "What are the metrics to say something is massive or niche?.... I feel like Tyler wins, because the metric is based upon his own personal success, not how it looks in one of these particular dimensions."[7]
> – Pharrell Williams

cop opens Felicia's trunk, he finds it overflowing with Mountain Dew bottles.

In the third commercial, Felicia is seen in a police lineup. The waitress from the first commercial, who is covered in bruises and using crutches, is meant to select her assailant from the lineup. Felicia threatens the waitress, saying, "Snitches get stitches," and "I'mma get out of here[, and] I'mma Dew you up."[5]

Many people found these commercials racist and misogynistic. Aside from the goat, the rest of the suspects in the lineup are black, dressed in saggy jeans and do-rags. Syracuse University professor Boyce Watkins called the commercial "arguably the most racist commercial in history."[6] Other people spoke about how the commercial made a joke out of women who were victims of assault or intimate partner violence because Felicia scares the woman away from picking him out of a lineup. Mountain Dew pulled the commercials after the third one was shown only one time.

Tyler defended his artistic viewpoint in many interviews afterward. His argument was the same as it had been in other controversies: people were applying meaning—in this case, racism and misogyny—to Tyler's videos when he did not put that meaning there. Tyler explained, "It's just a goat. I just think a goat is funny. It's no deeper meaning."[8] He even tweeted and then had a conversation with Watkins, who ultimately retracted some of his criticisms of Felicia.

While the scandal with Felicia ended Tyler's partnership with Mountain Dew, he didn't see it as a huge stumbling block

## FELICIA IN "TAMALE"

Shortly after the Mountain Dew controversy with Felicia the goat, Tyler released the music video for his song "Tamale." He referenced the controversy in an early scene of the video, which is purposefully censored and covered by the words "Due to the 'graphic nature' of this film, I was forced to blur because people aren't ready to have intelligent conversations before they judge. Welcome to America." Even though the scene is blurred, according to Tyler the shot features him in blackface makeup stomping around in a classroom with a friend. A portrait of Watkins hangs on the wall and watches as Felicia the goat runs past the boys. The next scene shows Tyler bouncing on a large woman's butt like a trampoline. It has the caption "But this s*** is allowed."[9] Tyler used the video to make a statement about which elements of his punk style and humor were seen as okay by the public and which elements were not.

65

toward fame and success. When pressed on whether the controversy would change Tyler's approach to art, he said, "I mean, it's not gonna change my art in any way."[10]

## OTHER CONTROVERSIES

Tyler's punk style worked in certain contexts, but the same humor that made him popular among his fans also made him a liability to his potential collaborators. While corporations wanted to work with Tyler and be associated with his offbeat content, they also feared being pulled over to the wrong side of the thin line he walked on controversial issues.

Tyler was feeling resistance in many of his creative pursuits. A T-shirt in his Golf Wang line sparked controversy, and even some of Tyler's Odd Future friends had issues with his

### TYLER PARTNERS WITH THE BEST

Tyler creates amazing products by partnering his art with the best products in the world. For example, he designed his puffy coats in collaboration with a company that works with the North Face and Patagonia. He partners with shoe and fashion companies that create products he already loves, such as Vans and Converse. Tyler gets to put his name on a quality product, and the company gets something too. Tyler said in an interview that companies he works with "trust that whatever art I put out, or whatever we collaborate on together, is gonna work."[11]

**Matt Martians performs with Syd Bennett as the band the Internet.**

creation. When Tyler designed a T-shirt featuring a person in blackface in his Golf Wang Fall/Winter 2013 lookbook, Syd Bennett and Matt Martians condemned the T-shirt, arguing that many of the people who would wear it would be white and that it was an irresponsible design.

Additionally, Tyler and other members of Odd Future were banned from performing in several countries. In August 2015, Tyler was turned away at the border of the United Kingdom. When he entered the country to

**Tyler and Odd Future had previously performed in the United Kingdom. In 2011, they performed at the Gaymers Camden Crawl festival in London.**

perform shows, he was led to a detention room and held for 30 minutes before being notified that he would not be allowed to enter the country for three to five years because of the offensive lyrics in his early songs. Prime Minister Theresa May stated that Tyler was a potential threat. A letter to Tyler's manager said the decision was based on the violent lyrics in *Bastard* and *Goblin*.

Though Tyler and Odd Future were moving past those lyrics, the old songs were still available on the internet. For the next few years, the members of Odd Future would have to deal with all kinds of blowback for their early work as they tried to take off in different directions.

## ODD FUTURE'S HYPNOTIC SOUND

Many journalists were wary of covering Odd Future early in the group's career because of its offensive lyrics. In an article about Odd Future in the *Guardian*, journalist Hermione Hoby mentioned being "hypnotised by the funk," which she defined as "[hearing] music whose content we object to, but whose sounds we can't help but respond to." Many journalists tried to look at the entirety of Odd Future, not just their lyrics. Hoby explained, "They're mocking white hipster expectations of black culture, or satirising rather than perpetuating hip-hop's ugliest recesses."[12]

# CHERRY BOMB AND THE DOCUMENTARY

*Chapter SEVEN*

After Tyler's South by Southwest performance and subsequent arrest in late 2014, some people wondered if that was the end of Odd Future. The group had experienced several months of hardship after rising quickly in popularity. In 2014, the Odd Future store on Fairfax shut down due to landlord issues. Tyler commented on how sad he was on the closing. "That was home base," he said. "I'm safe on that block." He added:

> I met a lot of friends [on Fairfax]. Travis, Thebe. Me and Jasper would go over there. There's a whole legion of younger kids like 15 or 16 that would hang around there so we like their big homies or whatever. That was a hangout spot for them and

Though Tyler had many setbacks in 2014 and 2015, his album *Cherry Bomb* was a hit with critics.

*it was good because it would kind of keep them out of trouble.*[1]

Then, at 2015's Camp Flog Gnaw, a fight erupted among the members of Odd Future. Band members shouted insults at each other from the stage. In 2015, it was widely believed that Odd Future had broken up because the members were all busy with their own bands, projects, and solo careers. They were moving in different directions. However, the 2015 lineup for Camp Flog Gnaw had listed OFWGKTA as a performer. Fans wondered who would show up for the time slot. Hodgy Beats, Domo Genesis, Left Brain, and Mike G. performed as

## MELLOWHYPE

Hodgy Beats created a duo called MellowHype with Left Brain. They signed to a small recording label in Mississippi called Fat Possum. The duo's first mixtape was titled *YelloWhite*. Their debut studio album was titled *BlackenedWhite*. The band later became a trio when fellow Odd Future member Domo Genesis joined them. In 2015, the three confirmed they were no longer together, but in 2017 they announced a reunion.

"With [Odd Future] it's a little bit more like a family. . . . You can beef and fight, but you can never split up because you're family. We don't always get along with one another, but you know you can come back."[2]

– Syd Tha Kyd

**Domo Genesis was one of the original members of Odd Future. In 2018, he performed at a tribute concert for rapper Mac Miller, who had died earlier that year.**

OFWGKTA, but Tyler and Earl Sweatshirt did not come out on stage.

    As Tyler watched from the side of the stage, Hodgy Beats trash-talked Tyler in front of the crowd. He called Tyler a fraud who didn't care about his Odd Future friends. Later, during his own set, Tyler shouted back, saying, "I helped too many of my . . . friends out. . . . And yes, this is real[.] I love you though."[3] A few days later, the old friends seemed to have made up. After a few days of commenting

> **Pharrell Williams performed at Camp Flog Gnaw in addition to collaborating on a *Cherry Bomb* track with Tyler.**

on each other's Instagram accounts, they said the beef was in the past.

## CHERRY BOMB

Tyler didn't have time to think too much about his past with OFWGKTA. He had an album, film, and book planned for 2015. His third studio album, *Cherry Bomb*, was released on April 13, 2015. The album debuted at Number 4 on the *Billboard* 200 charts. While it had the abrasive sounds that Tyler was known for, many critics praised the album for feeling exactly like what Tyler was good at. In a review of the album for *Pitchfork*, contributor Matthew Ramirez stated, "It's refreshing when an artist creates exactly the kind of art they want to create."[4]

> "Everyone is weird and crazy when you get to know them. [Tyler] displays that side of himself first. If you can get along with this side, you can get along with my other side."[5]
> – Lionel Boyce

*Cherry Bomb* featured A-list hip-hop collaborations from Kanye West, Lil Wayne, and Pharrell Williams—all artists who Tyler had looked up to as a teenager.

75

West, Lil Wayne, and Tyler all rap together on "Smuckers," which *Pitchfork* calls the album's best track. According to Ramirez, "With Tyler's verses bookending . . . the track and a beat switch thrown in the middle, it's as if he's playing hot potato with rap's most singular voices. . . . The thrilling part is how at home Kanye and Wayne sound having fun in this playground."[6]

## THE DOCUMENTARY AND BOOK

In 2015, Mikey Alfred, a teen filmmaker and friend of Tyler, filmed a 43-minute documentary called *Cherry Bomb: The Documentary*. It featured behind-the-scenes footage of Tyler writing and recording his album. The film was screened in January 2017 and was released in limited edition

### STRAIGHT EDGE

Tyler describes himself as straight edge. This means that he does not drink or do drugs. In *Cherry Bomb: The Documentary*, Tyler talks about his inspiration for the song "Run." According to Tyler, he woke up early and saw on social media that his friends were smoking marijuana at 9 o'clock. Later, in a recording session, Tyler told his friends to stop doing drugs while they were in the studio. He said, "This is a distraction. This needs to stop. We are here to f****** work. Not to hang out."[7] Tyler makes sure that his creative projects are the most important things in his life. Those projects include practicing on his skateboard and dirt bike. According to Tyler, he doesn't drink alcohol because it impairs his ability to jump over obstacles on his dirt bike.

**Much like Tyler, rapper A$AP Rocky also has an eclectic style and an interest in fashion.**

as a DVD, eventually becoming available via a streaming service. The film features appearances from musicians Kanye West, Lil Wayne, A$AP Rocky, and Frank Ocean, as well as composer Hans Zimmer.

**Ocean made several appearances in the *Cherry Bomb* documentary alongside other members of Odd Future.**

The movie itself looked like a Tyler video. Tyler speaks into a microphone, explaining how he comes up with and executes creative ideas. A$AP Rocky explains why he wants to work with the young rapper, as does Kanye West. In between interviews are scenes in the recording and production studios. Many of Tyler's songs feature breathy, light, melodic vocals from young artists. He also conducts a string section of orchestra musicians for the album. The artistic moments are interspersed with Tyler and his raucous friends riding in shopping carts and cracking each other up. The documentary makes it clear that having fun is still a part of Tyler's creative process.

> **TYLER AND SKATEBOARDING**
>
> Tyler wakes up early most days to write music at home, but he takes a lot of breaks and often plays video games and skateboards with his friends. In 2016, a game in the Tony Hawk's Pro Skater series made Tyler a playable character for PlayStation 4 and Xbox One. Players can choose to play as Tyler, who is dressed in Golf Wang brand clothes and skating on a yellow board that says GOLF.

    Tyler also published a 120-page book titled *GOLF BOOK* in 2015. The book included song lyrics from *Cherry Bomb*, as well as articles and interviews. Tyler wrote in the book that *Cherry Bomb* is his "most proud work and the only album [where] I really focused on the music instead of covering up the flaws with a bunch of characters."[8]

# FLOWER BOY AND *IGOR*

## Chapter EIGHT

Tyler's art and music were growing with him. In later interviews, Tyler curses less than he did in the Odd Future days. There is more nuance in his musings on art. Tyler's designs matured as he did. His travel and exposure to new experiences affected his style, as well as his aesthetic.

In 2016, MADE fashion week in Los Angeles featured the Golf Wang line as one of its main attractions. The event was even livestreamed to fans around the world. The show featured the gritty real-life aesthetic Tyler had cultivated as his signature. Instead of selecting models, he invited friends of all shapes and sizes to model the line. He even installed a skate ramp in the runway so guests could see his clothes in action doing activities that Tyler enjoyed.

When performing songs from *IGOR*, Tyler often wears a blonde wig.

## THE SUCCESS OF FLOWER BOY

Tyler's fourth studio album, *Flower Boy*, was released on July 21, 2017. It debuted at Number 2 on the *Billboard* 200 chart. The album had critics and fans talking not just about Tyler's music but also about the things he implied in his lyrics. Tyler himself has said he thinks it is his best album to date. He explains why: "I get all my points across. The features are done well. I found my version of writing a pop song but still a rap song. I still get weird musically, but it's not too gross."[1]

On *Flower Boy*, Tyler's lyrics teased at the possibility that he could be gay, and many fans wondered if the album was his way of coming out. Six years after the band had been scolded for homophobia in their lyrics, Tyler rapped on the song "I Ain't Got Time," "I been kissing white boys since 2004."[2] On two other songs on the

### GOLF WANG STORE

Things began to turn around for Tyler after the Odd Future store on Fairfax closed in 2014. In 2017, Tyler threw a huge party to celebrate when his Golf Wang flagship store opened, featuring Taco as DJ and appearances by several celebrities who have collaborated with Tyler in the past. Tyler designed the store, as well as all the clothes sold there.

album, he included lyrics about same-sex hookups. Some questioned whether Tyler was just goofing around about these references to his sexuality. Tyler had been known for being goofy so long it seemed plausible.

Tyler refused to comment on the buzz on his sexuality. "It's still such a gray area with people, which is cool with me. Even though I'm considered loud and out there, I'm private, which is a weird dichotomy. The juxtaposition of loud and quiet is weird."[3] On why he doesn't comment, he says, "The thing about humans is we hate not having an answer. We hate not being

### FAMILY-FRIENDLY PROJECTS

Between 2017 and 2018, Tyler worked on several family-friendly projects. He had always wanted to do more material for kids. Tyler worked with Hollywood composer Danny Elfman on the score of *The Grinch* (2018). After creating two songs for the soundtrack, he released an EP of six songs called *Music Inspired by Illumination & Dr. Seuss' The Grinch*. He also worked with scientist and TV host Bill Nye to create a theme song for the show *Bill Nye Saves the World*, which premiered on Netflix in 2017. In 2018, Tyler also appeared in an episode alongside Nye.

"I'm sporadic . . . but it works in my favor in the sense that I can multi-task well. . . . Luckily for me, the music and the clothes and the videos all play hand-in-hand."[4]

— Tyler, the Creator

**Tyler's tour for *Flower Boy* featured large, interactive onstage set pieces that he climbed around.**

in the know. . . . I don't know. There are some things that are just unexplainable."⁵ The album was received well by critics, earning a Grammy nomination for Best Rap Album in 2018.

The new view of homosexuality wasn't the only part of Tyler's music that seemed different from what came before. Critics noted that while the earlier music featured "confrontational verse, horror movie melodicism, [and] white hot rage," the newer music was "delicate and light,

## WORKING WITH FRANK OCEAN

Old friends Tyler and Ocean collaborated on the song "911" for Tyler's album *Flower Boy*. According to Tyler, he had already created a melody for the song when Ocean listened to it and said he didn't like it. Ocean started saying the word "chirp" over and over in order to convey his idea for a new melody. Tyler ended up adding a recording of Ocean saying "chirp, chirp, chirp" to the song. According to Tyler, his collaborations with Ocean are never planned but instead come organically out of listening to each other's work.

hooky."[6] In interviews, Tyler talks about how deeply personal this album was compared to his others. Several collaborators such as Ocean, Pharrell, and Estelle lent their vocals to the album.

## *IGOR*

Tyler announced his fifth studio solo album, *IGOR*, by tweet on May 6, 2019. He also tweeted possible cover art. The album dropped on May 17, 2019, and was met with critical acclaim.

The record debuted at Number 1 on the *Billboard* charts, a career first for Tyler. *IGOR* sold 165,000 albums in its first week. In addition, eight of the album's 12 tracks appeared on the *Billboard* Hot 100.[7] The *Independent* called the album Tyler's "best work to date."[8]

*Pitchfork* called *IGOR* "a perfectionist giving shape to his more radical ideas."[9] On the record, Tyler sings more than on his previous albums. During a concert, he revealed to fans that Kendrick Lamar made him feel more confident about his singing. He also included long instrumental sections without lyrics. He explained his

**Tyler performed his first single from *IGOR*, "EARFQUAKE," at the Governor's Ball music festival in New York City.**

reasoning: "A lot of the music that I love is instrumental. It made me realize, 'Oh, I don't always have to say something.' Sometimes we get caught up in filling voids that aren't even voids. That's just how it's supposed to be."[10]

The album showcases Tyler's ability to continuously evolve into something new, something closer to what he's been all along. In an article for *Billboard*, one critic said that *IGOR* was the truest version of Tyler that audiences had seen to date. Another critic explained, "Once he exuded a sense of openness within his music, beginning with *Flower Boy*, fans embraced him for his refreshing candor and have championed his newfound transparency. The more layers he continues to peel back, the more receptive his audience will be."[11]

## "EARFQUAKE" SHAKE UP

One of the first singles from *IGOR*, "EARFQUAKE," features Charlie Wilson and Playboi Carti. Originally, when Tyler wrote the song in May 2017, he imagined it would go to Justin Bieber. However, Bieber turned it down. Tyler also offered the song to Rihanna, but she passed on it too. Tyler then recorded the song himself and released it on *IGOR*. After an earthquake struck California on July 4, 2019, #earfquake became a trending hashtag. People used the hashtag to talk about both the natural disaster and Tyler's new album.

However, not everyone loved *IGOR*. Hip-hop artist DJ Khaled took a shot at Tyler the week that *IGOR* hit Number 1 on the *Billboard* charts, because it made Khaled's album debut in the Number 2 spot. Khaled posted a video to social media, complaining that he deserved the Number 1 spot because he makes "albums so that people can play it and you actually hear it . . . not no mysterious s***, and you never hear it." Tyler responded with a tweet: "HIS MSG [Madison Square Garden] SHOW SOLD OUT BUT FR [for real] I NEVER HEARD A TYLER SONG IN MY LIFE," followed by three laughing emoji.[12]

> "My core is to explore. That curiosity, people lose that, because they think they know everything."[13]
>
> – Tyler, the Creator

In June 2019, Tyler announced by tweet the dates of a world tour in support of *IGOR*, including stops in the United Kingdom. As of 2019, Tyler is no longer banned from the United Kingdom. This opened up Tyler to new audiences, fans who have long clamored to get closer to Tyler. He was beginning to overcome the missteps of his earlier albums and fine-tune his sound.

# THE FUTURE OF TYLER

*Chapter NINE*

It's impossible to say what Tyler will do next. He revels in surprising audiences with his innovative approaches to music, art, and fashion. No matter what trail he takes, Tyler, the Creator will forever be associated with a crowd of goofballs and artists in the collective of musicians and artists known as Odd Future.

Tyler, the Creator infiltrated the world of rap while maintaining his unique perspective and ultimate control over his artistic vision. This is a big accomplishment in an industry notorious for labeling artists and then chewing them up and spitting them out.

Tyler broke into the industry not through the standard channels but by putting his own work out there for the public through YouTube, Tumblr, and later, Odd Future's own proprietary Golf Media app. He gave his content away for free, appealing to kids just like him, who were

Tyler sported an eclectic outfit at the 2018 Grammy Awards.

longing for something real. He's admired not only by young people who want to rap and create art but also by young entrepreneurs. Young misfits enjoy his perspective and his honesty.

## FUTURE OF TYLER'S MUSIC

Over the course of his career, Tyler has become a more introspective artist. Some reviewers call *IGOR* a "breakup album," as if Tyler is letting go of his old ways and

**Tyler's growth from *Goblin* to *IGOR* shows the development of his personal style in both music and fashion.**

embracing new ideas.[1] Christian Clancy credits Tyler's broadening horizons and more evolved sound to "life experience, touring the world, [his] own evolution as a human being, and exposure to a wider world."[2] The kid who used to look up to André 3000 now chats with him regularly and trades artwork with him.

However, despite studio backing, Tyler still prefers to announce his new albums via his personal Twitter shortly before they are released. Tyler's approach disrupts a music industry that is used to large promotional launches and orchestrated career moves. One certainty for the future is that Tyler will continue to collaborate with other artists. In 2019, he appeared on the song "Castaway" by Malaysian artist Yuna. He also collaborated with rapper GoldLink on his song "U Say."

### NUTS + BOLTS

Tyler hosted a reality series for the Viceland network called *Nuts + Bolts*. In the documentary-style show, Tyler talked about things that interested him, and then he worked alongside experts in the industry to learn the whole story on how they work. Over the course of the episodes, Tyler's creations came to life. Tyler did shows on topics like stop-motion photography, furniture building, go-kart design, and therapeutic floating. He also documented his collaboration with Converse to design limited edition One Star shoes.

Tyler attended the 2019 French Open tennis tournament. He used the opportunity to promote his new fashion line.

## CHANNEL ORANGE

Tyler made an appearance on Ocean's 2012 album, *Channel Orange*. He rapped on "Golden Girl," a bonus track only available on the physical copy of *Channel Orange*. Tyler is listed as a writer and producer on other songs on the album, including a collaboration with guitarist John Mayer. Ocean and his collaborators were nominated for six Grammys for the album, including 2012 Album of the Year.

> "[Producing is] all I want to do. . . . I'm gonna spend the next two years, probably working on clothes and just producing for others. . . . I want to go, 'You want pop s***? You want rap?'"[3]
> —Tyler, the Creator

## FUTURE OF FASHION

Tyler continues to branch out into new concepts with fashion labels while still remaining true to his individual sense of style. Tyler designed a Golf le Fleur* line of clothes with the Lacoste label that was released in July 2019. In early video and promotional images showcasing the line, Tyler can be seen in the background, his face hidden behind a retro-style camera.

He also worked with Lacoste to create a tennis-inspired menswear line. He modeled the line by wearing pieces to the 2019 French Open. In an

**Tyler's other projects, such as working on the soundtrack for 2018's remake of *The Grinch*, have inspired his own music.**

article for *GQ*, a reviewer described the line as "youthful but polished, not unlike a frame from a Wes Anderson film." The article also noted that the line "speaks volumes of how far the designer has come—and how much further he's headed."[4]

## OTHER SIDE PROJECTS

Proving that he can add his flair to pretty much any product, in 2019, Tyler partnered with Jeni's Splendid Ice Creams to create his own flavor of ice cream. The flavor was called Snowflake. A press release described the two-tone ice cream as "cool peppermint on the ivory side, warm spearmint on the green side, with buttery white chocolate melted throughout, white chocolate flakes for some crunch, and a little sea salt to bring the flavor and scent forward."⁵ The ice cream could be purchased in-store at Tyler's GOLF locations, as well as online on both Jeni's and GOLF's websites. Tyler also created a GOLF Snowflake T-shirt to accompany the ice cream launch.

> ### BECOMING
>
> In 2017, Tyler wrote the music for a short film called *Becoming* by Portland artist Aminé. The film is about the artist's musical ambitions when he was in high school. Aminé, who has a distinctive appearance and a penchant for wearing bright colors, has been compared to Tyler by critics. The film featured actors playing Aminé and his friends when they were in high school. Tyler's original music played during the closing credits.

Tyler is an example to all young artists and entrepreneurs. His career teaches two great lessons for anyone interested in crafting a creative career: Always be yourself, and keep as much ownership of your art as possible. There is no telling what Tyler will do next, but it will probably be weird, innovative, and brightly colored.

# TIMELINE

## 1991
Tyler is born in Los Angeles, California, on March 6.

## 2008
Odd Future releases its debut project, *The Odd Future Tape Vol. 1*, on November 16.

## 2009
Tyler releases the free digital album *Bastard* on December 25.

## 2011
In February, Tyler, the Creator releases the groundbreaking video for "Yonkers."

In April, Odd Future creates Odd Future Records.

Tyler releases his first studio album, *Goblin*, on May 10, through XL Records.

Tyler is nominated for two VMAs for Best New Artist and Video of the Year for "Yonkers." He wins the VMA for Best New Artist.

## 2012
The first Camp Flog Gnaw is held on September 30.

Odd Future releases *The OF Tape Vol. 2* on March 20.

On March 25, Odd Future's sketch comedy show *Loiter Squad* premieres on Cartoon Network's Adult Swim.

## 2013
Tyler releases his second studio album, *Wolf*, on April 2.

Tyler is nominated for a Grammy for Album of the Year for his work on *Channel Orange*.

## 2014
In March, Tyler is arrested for inciting a riot at SXSW.

Tyler is nominated for a VMA for Best Art Direction for his video "Tamale."

## 2015

Tyler releases his third studio album, *Cherry Bomb*, on April 13.

Tyler publishes a book of Odd Future images called *GOLF BOOK*.

Tyler announces that *Loiter Squad* is ending its run on Adult Swim.

In August, Tyler is turned away from the UK border based on his lyrics and is forced to cancel shows.

Tyler launches the Golf Media app, made exclusively for Odd Future content.

## 2016

Tyler's brand Golf Wang appears at a runway show in Los Angeles.

Camp Flog Gnaw becomes a two-day event for the first time.

## 2017

On July 10, Tyler reveals his first collaboration with Converse sneakers.

Tyler, the Creator's fourth studio album, *Flower Boy*, is released on July 21.

## 2018

Tyler contributes two songs to the soundtrack for *The Grinch*.

*Flower Boy* is nominated for a Grammy for Best Rap Album.

Tyler creates a theme song for the Netflix show *Bill Nye Saves the World*.

## 2019

Tyler releases his fifth studio album, *IGOR*, on May 17.

## ESSENTIAL FACTS

### FULL NAME
Tyler Gregory Okonma

### DATE OF BIRTH
March 6, 1991

### PLACE OF BIRTH
Los Angeles, California

### PARENT
Bonita Smith

### EDUCATION
Attended Media Art Academy in Hawthorne, California

### CAREER HIGHLIGHTS
Tyler, the Creator founded the hip-hop collective Odd Future while still in high school. The group began posting videos and photos online on various social media platforms. In 2011, Tyler won a VMA for Best New Artist for the video for "Yonkers." Since then, he has been nominated for several other awards, including a Grammy for his work on Frank Ocean's 2012 album, *Channel Orange*, as well as for Tyler's own album *Flower Boy*. In 2019, Tyler's album *IGOR* debuted at Number 1 on the *Billboard* charts.

### ALBUMS
*Bastard* (2009), *Goblin* (2011), *Wolf* (2013), *Cherry Bomb* (2015), *Flower Boy* (2017), *Music Inspired by Illumination & Dr. Seuss' The Grinch* (2018), *IGOR* (2019)

## CONTRIBUTION TO HIP-HOP

Tyler, the Creator is credited with changing how the music game is played. While historically musicians had to sign with a label to reach their fans, Tyler reversed the approach. He attracted legions of fans by giving his music away for free on the internet. Soon, the music industry approached him, with producers fighting among themselves to get his attention. He encourages artists to own the rights to their creative products so they can continue to profit from their work, instead of giving up a majority of their profits to record companies and corporations.

## CONFLICTS

- Tyler was a brash teenager, rapping about rape and violence at the start of his career. While Tyler's abrasive and offensive mystique attracted fans to him in the beginning, the lyrics have also caused him a lot of trouble. Some countries banned Tyler from visiting because they believed he created work with the intention of inciting violence and misogynistic behavior.

- Tyler publicly argued with Odd Future member Hodgy Beats at Camp Flog Gnaw in 2015; however, the old friends made up within days. He also feuded with DJ Khaled after Tyler's album *IGOR* debuted at Number 1 on the *Billboard* charts and Khaled's album debuted at Number 2.

## QUOTE

"I wanted to do something cool. It's always about me doing something that I think is awesome."

—*Tyler, the Creator*

# GLOSSARY

### AESTHETIC
A set of ideas or opinions about beauty or art.

### ALTER EGO
A persona that an artist might use for different projects.

### COLLABORATION
Multiple artists working together on a single track or album.

### COLLECTIVE
A group of people working together.

### ENTREPRENEUR
A person who organizes and operates a business or businesses.

### LIABILITY
A person or thing that is likely to cause trouble, embarrassment, or some other kind of negative effect.

## LOOKBOOK
A collection of photographs assembled to show off the work of a clothing line.

## MANTRA
A statement that people repeat over and over.

## MISOGYNY
Hatred of or contempt for women.

## ROYALTY
A share of money generated by sales of a work.

## SOUNDTRACK
A collection of music that accompanies a film.

## SPONSORSHIP
Financial support from a company given to complete a project.

## VIDEOGRAPHER
A person who produces films.

# ADDITIONAL RESOURCES

## SELECTED BIBLIOGRAPHY

Caramanica, Jon. "Angry Rhymes, Dirty Mouth, Goofy Kid." *New York Times*, 4 May 2011, nytimes.com. Accessed 11 Mar. 2019.

Trammell, Matthew. "Tyler, the Creator: A Young Boss Grows Up on His Own Terms." *Fader*, 9 Nov. 2014, thefader.com. Accessed 25 Mar. 2019.

Zellner, Xander. "13 Things to Know about the Charts This Week: Tyler, the Creator Earns First Billboard 200 No. 1 & Biggest Hot 100 Hit." *Billboard*, 1 June 2019, billboard.com. Accessed 12 June 2019.

## FURTHER READINGS

Burling, Alexis. *Pharrell Williams: Grammy-Winning Singer, Songwriter & Producer*. Abdo, 2015.

Morris, Rebecca. *Hip-Hop Groups*. Abdo, 2018.

## ONLINE RESOURCES

To learn more about Tyler, the Creator, please visit abdobooklinks.com or scan this QR code. These links are routinely monitored and updated to provide the most current information available.

## MORE INFORMATION

For more information on this subject, contact or visit the following organizations:

### CAMP FLOG GNAW
campfloggnaw.com

Camp Flog Gnaw is an annual carnival presented by Tyler, the Creator and the other members of Odd Future. Guests can watch musical performances, play carnival games, and shop for merch that is all curated by Tyler.

### DISCOVER LOS ANGELES
discoverlosangeles.com

Discover Los Angeles is the website of the tourism board for Los Angeles, California. People can find local events, concerts, hotels, and more.

### SONY MUSIC
25 Madison Ave.
New York, NY 10010
sonymusic.com

Sony Music is a record label that distributes Tyler, the Creator's music. The label's other signed artists include Travis Scott, Mark Ronson, and Camila Cabello.

# SOURCE NOTES

## CHAPTER 1. RIOT IN AUSTIN, TEXAS

1. Chase Hoffberger. "Tyler, the Creator: A Timeline of the Rapper's Notorious SXSW." *Austin Chronicle*, 18 Mar. 2014, austinchronicle.com. Accessed 20 Mar. 2019.

2. Hoffberger, "Tyler, the Creator."

3. Evan Minsker. "Tyler, the Creator Arrested for Inciting a Riot at SXSW." *Pitchfork*, 15 Mar. 2014, pitchfork.com. Accessed 27 Aug. 2019.

4. Jem Aswad. "Tyler, the Creator Arrested for Inciting Riot at SXSW." *Spin*, 15 Mar. 2014, spin.com. Accessed 21 Mar. 2019.

5. "Rapper Tyler, the Creator Arrested at South by Southwest." *Fox News*, 14 Mar. 2014, foxnews.com. Accessed 27 Aug. 2019.

6. Jazmine Ulloa. "As Rapper's Riot Charge Is Dropped, Legal Experts Question Arrest." *Austin American-Statesman*, 16 Aug. 2016, statesman.com. Accessed 20 Mar. 2019.

7. "Tyler, the Creator Charged with Inciting a Riot at SXSW." *CBS News*, 17 Mar. 2014, cbsnews.com. Accessed 8 Mar. 2019.

8. Julianne Escobedo Shepherd. "Odd Future's Tyler, the Creator on Race, Broken Homes, and Waking Up Rich." *Spin*, 21 Nov. 2011, spin.com. Accessed 27 Aug. 2019.

9. Hoffberger, "Tyler, the Creator."

10. Shepherd, "Odd Future's Tyler, the Creator."

## CHAPTER 2. EARLY LIFE

1. Mitchell Landsberg. "Students Get a Last Chance—Rap." *Los Angeles Times*, 19 Jan. 2008, latimes.com. Accessed 10 Mar. 2019.

2. Julianne Escobedo Shepherd. "Odd Future's Tyler, the Creator on Race, Broken Homes, and Waking Up Rich." *Spin*, 21 Nov. 2011, spin.com. Accessed 27 Aug. 2019.

3. Shepherd, "Odd Future's Tyler, the Creator."

4. Jon Caramanica. "Angry Rhymes, Dirty Mouth, Goofy Kid." *New York Times*, 4 May 2011, nytimes.com. Accessed 11 Mar. 2019.

5. Alex Frank. "Why You'll Want to Be Online Sunday before Tyler, the Creator's New Collection Sells Out." *Vogue*, 11 Dec. 2015, vogue.com. Accessed 27 Aug. 2019.

6. Landsberg, "Students Get a Last Chance."

7. Matthew Strauss. "Read Tyler, the Creator's Long Essay on Pharrell's *In My Mind* for 10th Anniversary." *Pitchfork*, 25 July 2016, pitchfork.com. Accessed 27 Aug. 2019.

8. Landsberg, "Students Get a Last Chance."

9. Joshua Espinoza. "Tyler, the Creator Explains Why He Changed His Infamous Twitter Handle." *Complex*, 29 Aug. 2016, complex.com. Accessed 27 Aug. 2019.

10. "James Pants." *Stones Throw*, n.d., stonesthrow.com. Accessed 27 Aug. 2019.

## CHAPTER 3. THE EARLY DAYS OF ODD FUTURE

1. "Read: Casen Kreation Interviews Tyler, the Creator." *Respect*, 25 Dec. 2011, respect-mag.com. Accessed 14 Mar. 2019.

2. Harriet Gibsone. "Syd: 'The Backlash from the Gay Community Hurt My Feelings.'" *Guardian*, 30 May 2017, theguardian.com. Accessed 27 Aug. 2019.

3. Sonaiya Kelley. "A Hip-Hop Game Changer: How Grammy-Nominated Tyler, the Creator Became Tyler, the Entrepreneur." *Los Angeles Times*, 26 Jan. 2018, latimes.com. Accessed 27 Aug. 2019.

4. "Tyler, the Creator: *Bastard*." *Genius*, 25 Dec. 2009, genius.com. Accessed 14 Mar. 2019.

5. "How They Came Up. The Tyler the Creator Story." *Indiehiphop.net*, 31 Oct. 2011, indiehiphop.net. Accessed 17 July 2019.

6. Mark Wilson. "Tyler, the Creator Is in Full Bloom." *Fast Company*, 18 Oct. 2018, fastcompany.com. Accessed 9 Mar. 2019.

7. Wilson, "Tyler, the Creator Is in Full Bloom."

## CHAPTER 4. "THE VIDEO OF 2011"

1. "Tyler, the Creator." *Wonderland*, 1 July 2011, wonderlandmagazine.com. Accessed 10 Mar. 2019.

2. Zach Kelly. "Yonkers." *Pitchfork*, 14 Feb. 2011, pitchfork.com. Accessed 17 July 2019.

3. "Tyler, the Creator: Yonkers." *Genius*, n.d., genius.com. Accessed 27 Aug. 2019.

4. Kelly, "Yonkers."

5. Tom Breihan. "Odd Future's Earl Sweatshirt: Found?" *Pitchfork*, 14 Apr. 2011, pitchfork.com. Accessed 27 Aug. 2019.

6. Nick Harwood. "Tyler, and the Creators of Yonkers." *Respect*, 12 July 2011, respect-mag.com. Accessed 10 Mar. 2019.

7. Ryan Schreiber. "Watch: Odd Future's Insane 'Fallon' Performance." *Pitchfork*, 17 Feb. 2011, pitchfork.com. Accessed 11 Mar. 2019.

8. Schreiber, "Watch: Odd Future's Insane 'Fallon' Performance."

9. Colin Stutz. "Frank Ocean Explains His Decision to Sit Out 2017 Grammys." *Billboard*, 15 Nov. 2016, billboard.com. Accessed 27 Aug. 2019.

10. Mark Wilson. "Tyler, the Creator Is in Full Bloom." *Fast Company*, 18 Oct. 2018, fastcompany.com. Accessed 9 Mar. 2019.

11. Andres Tardio. "OFWGKTA All Bypass Major Labels for Sony Distribution, Signing Themselves." *Hip Hop DX*, 26 Apr. 2011, hiphopdx.com. Accessed 23 Mar. 2019.

12. Jon Caramanica. "Angry Rhymes, Dirty Mouth, Goofy Kid." *New York Times*, 4 May 2011, nytimes.com. Accessed 11 Mar. 2019.

13. Kelefa Sanneh. "Where's Earl?" *New Yorker*, 16 May 2011, newyorker.com. Accessed 27 Aug. 2019.

14. Jason Lipshutz. "Tyler, the Creator Wins Best New Artist VMA." *Billboard*, 29 Aug. 2011, billboard.com. Accessed 13 Mar. 2019.

## CHAPTER 5. BRANCHING INTO NEW PROJECTS

1. Alex Frank. "Why You'll Want to Be Online Sunday before Tyler, the Creator's New Collection Sells Out." *Vogue*, 11 Dec. 2015, vogue.com. Accessed 27 Aug. 2019.

2. "News: Tyler, the Creator—'I Am About to Be a Good Person for Once.'" *Respect*, 19 June 2013, respect-mag.com. Accessed 27 Aug. 2019.

3. Alex Myers. "Why Tyler, the Creator Created the Hottest-Selling 'Golf' Clothing Line When He Doesn't Even Like Golf." *Golf Digest*, 9 Dec. 2015, golfdigest.com. Accessed 27 Aug. 2019.

4. Myers, "Why Tyler, the Creator Created the Hottest-Selling 'Golf' Clothing Line."

5. Emily Manning. "Tyler, the Creator Is Rewriting Fashion's Rulebook in Neon." *Vice*, 30 Sept. 2016, vice.com. Accessed 21 Mar. 2019.

6. Frank, "Why You'll Want to Be Online."

7. "Odd Future Announce Los Angeles Carnival." *Pitchfork*, 17 Aug. 2012, pitchfork.com. Accessed 15 July 2019.

8. Julian Mitchell. "Camp Flog Gnaw: The Business Behind Tyler the Creator's Immersive Music Festival." *Forbes*, 27 Nov. 2019, forbes.com. Accessed 21 Mar. 2019.

9. Chris Mench. "A Lyrical Analysis of Queer Themes in Frank Ocean's Music." *Genius*, 15 Mar. 2017, genius.com. Accessed 27 Aug. 2019.

# SOURCE NOTES CONTINUED

10. Gil Kaufman. "Frank Ocean Gets Support from Tyler, the Creator, Russell Simmons on Coming Out." *MTV*, 5 July 2012, mtv.com. Accessed 22 Mar. 2019.
11. Mitchell, "Camp Flog Gnaw."
12. Mitchell, "Camp Flog Gnaw."
13. Mark Wilson. "Tyler, the Creator Is in Full Bloom." *Fast Company*, 18 Oct. 2018, fastcompany.com. Accessed 9 Mar. 2019.
14. Denise Petski. "Tyler the Creator & Lionel Boyce Ink First-Look Deal with Sony Pictures TV." *Deadline*, 17 Oct. 2018, deadline.com. Accessed 27 Aug. 2019.
15. Sonaiya Kelley. "A Hip-Hop Game Changer: How Grammy-Nominated Tyler, the Creator Became Tyler, the Entrepreneur." *Los Angeles Times*, 26 Jan. 2018, latimes.com. Accessed 27 Aug. 2019.
16. Evan Minsker. "Tyler, the Creator Launches Golf Media App." *Pitchfork*, 8 Apr. 2015, pitchfork.com. Accessed 27 Aug. 2019.

### CHAPTER 6. TYLER TRIES TO GROW

1. Christopher Harris. "Tyler, the Creator: 'I'm Borderline Genius.'" *HipHopDX*, 17 Apr. 2015, hiphopdx.com. Accessed 27 Aug. 2019.
2. Rob Tannenbaum. "Q&A: Tyler, the Creator." *Rolling Stone*, 11 Apr. 2013, rollingstone.com. Accessed 15 Mar. 2019.
3. Craig Jenkins. "Tyler, the Creator: *Wolf*." *Pitchfork*, 1 Apr. 2013, pitchfork.com. Accessed 27 Aug. 2019.
4. Chris Martins. "In Defense of Tyler, the Creator's Bear-Poking 'Tamale' Video." *Spin*, 8 Oct. 2013, spin.com. Accessed 27 Aug. 2019.
5. "Mountain Dew Commercial by Tyler the Creator." *Daily Motion*, n.d., dailymotion.com. Accessed 27 Aug. 2019.
6. Julianne Escobedo Shepherd. "Tyler, the Creator Talks Mountain Dew Controversy." *Billboard*, 2 May 2013, billboard.com. Accessed 23 Mar. 2019.
7. Mark Wilson. "Tyler, the Creator Is in Full Bloom." *Fast Company*, 18 Oct. 2018, fastcompany.com. Accessed 9 Mar. 2019.
8. Eric R. Danton. "Tyler, the Creator Responds to Criticism of Mountain Dew Ad." *Rolling Stone*, 3 May 2013, rollingstone.com. Accessed 27 Aug. 2019.
9. Tyler, the Creator. "Tamale." *YouTube*, uploaded by OFWGKTA, 7 Oct. 2013, youtube.com. Accessed 28 Aug. 2019.
10. Shepherd, "Tyler, the Creator Talks Mountain Dew Controversy."
11. Wilson, "Tyler, the Creator Is in Full Bloom."
12. Hermione Hoby. "Rappers and Rape: The Incredible Sound and Hateful Lyrics of Odd Future." *Guardian*, 7 May 2011, theguardian.com. Accessed 27 Aug. 2019.

### CHAPTER 7. CHERRY BOMB AND THE DOCUMENTARY

1. Victoria Hernandez. "Tyler, the Creator Explains What's Wrong with Music Today." *HipHopDX*, 8 Apr. 2015, hiphopdx.com. Accessed 20 Mar. 2019.
2. Matthew Trammell. "No, Odd Future Don't Hate Each Other." *Fader*, 28 May 2015, thefader.com. Accessed 28 Aug. 2019.
3. "Tyler the Creator and Hodgy Beats Fight as Odd Future Continues to Disintegrate." *Pitchfork*, 16 Nov. 2015, pitchfork.com. Accessed 19 Mar. 2019.
4. Matthew Ramirez. "Tyler, the Creator: *Cherry Bomb*." *Pitchfork*, 17 Apr. 2015, pitchfork.com. Accessed 28 Aug. 2019.
5. Mark Wilson. "Tyler, the Creator Is in Full Bloom." *Fast Company*, 18 Oct. 2018, fastcompany.com. Accessed 9 Mar. 2019.
6. Ramirez, "Tyler, the Creator: *Cherry Bomb*."

7. Paul Flynn. "Tyler, the Creator." *Fantastic Man*, Autumn/Winter 2018, fantasticman.com. Accessed 28 Aug. 2019.

8. Tyler, the Creator. *GOLF BOOK*. Tyler, the Creator, 2015. 1.

## CHAPTER 8. *FLOWER BOY* AND *IGOR*

1. Paul Flynn. "Popular Culture with Tyler, the Creator." *Fantastic Man*, Autumn/Winter 2018, fantasticman.com. Accessed 28 Aug. 2019.

2. Craig Jenkins. "Tyler, the Obfuscator." *New York*, 7–20 Aug. 2017, nymag.com. Accessed 28 Aug. 2019.

3. Flynn, "Popular Culture with Tyler, the Creator."

4. Emily Manning. "Tyler, the Creator Is Rewriting Fashion's Rulebook in Neon." *Vice*, 30 Sept. 2016, vice.com. Accessed 28 Aug. 2019.

5. Flynn, "Popular Culture with Tyler, the Creator."

6. Craig Jenkins. "The Personal Reckoning of Tyler, the Creator's *Flower Boy*." *Vulture*, 28 July 2017, vulture.com. Accessed 28 Aug. 2019.

7. FNR TIGG, "8 Songs from Tyler, the Creator's *IGOR* Have Entered the Hot 100." *Complex*, 28 May 2019, complex.com. Accessed 28 Aug. 2019.

8. Roisin O'Connor. "Tyler, the Creator Review, *IGOR*: His Best Work to Date." *Independent*, 17 May 2019, independent.co.uk. Accessed 28 Aug. 2019.

9. Matthew Strauss. "Tyler, the Creator: *IGOR*." *Pitchfork*, 20 May 2019, pitchfork.com. Accessed 28 Aug. 2019.

10. Eric Skelton. "Everything We Learned from Tyler, the Creator's First Performance of *IGOR*." *Complex*, 23 May 2019, complex.com. Accessed 28 Aug. 2019.

11. "Five Burning Questions: Tyler, the Creator's Career Week on the Charts with *IGOR*." *Billboard*, 31 May 2019, billboard.com. Accessed 28 Aug. 2019.

12. "DJ Khaled Brags about Beating Tyler, the Creator during 2nd Sales Week." *YouTube*, uploaded by HipHopDX, 12 June 2019, youtube.com. Accessed 28 Aug. 2019.

13. Mark Wilson. "Tyler, the Creator Is in Full Bloom." *Fast Company*, 18 Oct. 2018, fastcompany.com. Accessed 9 Mar. 2019.

## CHAPTER 9. THE FUTURE OF TYLER

1. John Cotter. "*IGOR*: The Break-Up Album that Proves Tyler, the Creator Belongs in a Category All His Own." *DePaulia*, 3 June 2019, depauliaonline.com. Accessed 28 Aug. 2019.

2. "Rap Radar: Christian Clancy." *YouTube*, uploaded by Tidal, 15 June 2019, youtube.com. Accessed 28 Aug. 2019.

3. James Rettig. "Tyler, the Creator Wants to Work with Billie Eilish." *Stereogum*, 18 July 2019, stereogum.com. Accessed 28 Aug. 2019.

4. Tyler Watamanuk. "Tyler, the Creator and Lacoste Make Tennis Clothes for the Menswear Crowd." *GQ*, 10 July 2019, gq.com. Accessed 28 Aug. 2019.

5. Matthew Strauss. "Tyler, the Creator Unveils Signature Ice Cream Flavor." *Pitchfork*, 1 July 2019, pitchfork.com. Accessed 28 Aug. 2019.

# INDEX

Adult Swim, 54–56, 57, 59
Alfred, Mikey, 76
André 3000, 18, 20, 93
asthma, 12

*Bastard*, 31, 61, 69
Beats, Hodgy, 25, 39–40, 61, 72–73
*Becoming*, 97
Bennett, Syd, 26–28, 67
*Bill Nye Saves the World*, 83
*Billboard* charts, 61, 75, 82, 86, 89
Boyce, Lionel, 23, 56, 57, 59, 75

Camp Flog Gnaw, 52–53, 72
Campbell, Kareem, 16
Cartoon Network, 53–54, 56, 58
*Channel Orange*, 52, 94
charity, 48
*Cherry Bomb*, 75, 76, 79
Clancy, Christian, 31–32, 36, 40, 42, 47–48, 93
controversial lyrics, 18, 26, 28, 52, 66, 69
Converse, 51, 66, 93
critical reception, 20, 31–32, 35–37, 40, 43, 61–62, 69, 75, 84–86, 88

DJ Khaled, 89

"EARFQUAKE," 88
Earl Sweatshirt, 29, 37, 43, 61, 73
early life, 15–23
Elfman, Danny, 83
Eminem, 12, 32

Fallon, Jimmy, 39
fashion, 18, 23, 48–51, 66, 81, 91, 94–96
Felicia the goat commercials, 62–66
*Flower Boy*, 82–84, 86, 88

Genesis, Domo, 23, 72
*Goblin*, 39, 40, 43, 69
GoldLink, 93
*GOLF BOOK*, 79
Golf le Fleur*, 51, 94
Golf Media app, 56–59, 91
Golf Wang, 48–50, 66–67, 79, 81, 82
Golf Wang store, 82
*Grinch, The*, 83

homophobia, 18, 26, 28, 52, 82

ice cream, 96–97
*IGOR*, 20, 86–89, 92
Internet, the (band), 28

*Jellies, The*, 57–59

Kgositsile, Keorapetse, 43

Lacoste, 94
Ladera Heights, Los Angeles, 15, 19
Lamar, Kendrick, 87
Lil Wayne, 75–76, 77
*Loiter Squad*, 50, 56–57

MADE fashion week, 81
Mandler, Anthony, 36
Martians, Matt, 25, 28, 67
May, Theresa, 69
Media Art Academy, 20–23
MellowHype, 72
Minton, Perry, 10
misogyny, 28, 64–65
MTV Video Music Awards, 37, 44, 62
MySpace, 20, 27

New Zealand, 12
Newman, Walter J., 55
*Nuts + Bolts*, 93

Ocean, Frank, 29, 42, 52, 77, 86, 94
Odd Future, 10, 13, 20, 21, 23, 25–33, 35–36, 37, 39–45, 47–50, 52–56, 61, 66–69, 71–73, 81, 82, 91
Odd Future Records, 28, 40–42, 61
Odd Future Store, 50, 71, 82
*OF Tape, Vol. 2, The*, 42
OFWGKTA Carnival, 52
Outkast, 20

Pants, James, 21
*Pitchfork*, 29, 31, 35, 36, 61, 75, 76, 86

Rihanna, 88

skateboarding, 5, 16, 20, 23, 25, 29, 50, 76, 79
Smith, Bonita, 15, 18, 19, 45
Sony Pictures TV, 56
Sony Records, 42
South by Southwest (SXSW), 5–13

"Tamale," 62, 65
*Thrasher*, 5
*Tony Hawk's Pro Skater*, 16, 79
Tremaine, Jeff, 56
Tumblr, 31, 39, 40, 52, 91
Twitter, 37, 93

United Kingdom, 67–69, 89

Vans, 47, 50–51, 57, 66
violent lyrics, 18, 26, 28, 69

Watkins, Boyce, 64–65
Wattles, Kevin, 53
West, Kanye, 18, 37, 75–77, 79
Williams, Pharrell, 10, 20, 51, 64, 75
*Wolf*, 61–62

XL Recordings, 35

"Yonkers," 35–37, 39, 40
YouTube, 25, 39, 42, 91
Yuna, 93

111

## ABOUT THE AUTHOR

Marie Jaskulka writes poetry, fiction, and nonfiction for teens and adults. She is the author of *The Lost Marble Notebook of Forgotten Girl & Random Boy*. She grew up in Philadelphia and now lives in northeastern Pennsylvania, where she enjoys attending concerts, traveling, and trying just about anything once.